IF FOUND PLEASE KINDLY RETURN TO:

NAME:

_____

CELL:

_____

THE ENNEAGRAM PRAYER JOURNAL

Created to remind
you of God's Goodness
in every season.

Published by Journal Hub
Los Angeles, California

Copyright © My Prayer Journal 2019

Scripture quotations marked (NIV) are taken from the THE HOLY BIBLE, NEW INTERNATIONAL VERSION®, NIV® Copyright © 1973, 1978, 1984, 2011 by Biblica, Inc.™ Used by permission. All rights reserved worldwide.

If you are interested in bulk orders for your church or organization, message us at enneagramjournal.co/contact

Lets get Personal.

Who does this journal belong to?

_____

What does your relationship with Jesus look like?

_____

How often do you pray?

_____

City & State you live in?

_____

Do you currently attend a church? If so, what do you love about it?

_____

Group of friends that you will journal with to keep accountable to:

_____

WHAT IS THE ENNEAGRAM?

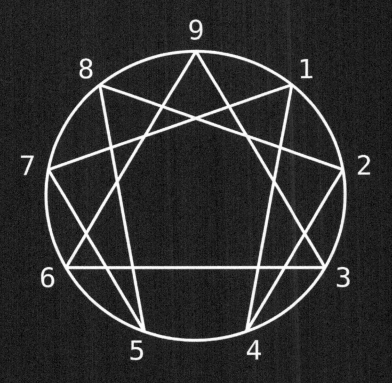

The Enneagram is a personality typing system that consists of nine different types. Everyone is considered to be one single type, although one can have traits belonging to other ones.

While it's uncertain whether this type is genetically determined, many believe it is already in place at birth.

The nine types (or "enneatypes", "ennea" means "nine") are universally identified by the numbers 1 to 9.

These numbers have a standard way of being placed around the Enneagram symbol. Enneagram authors have attached their own individual names to these numbers they are as follows:

1. The Reformer
2. The Helper
3. The Achiever
4. The Individualist
5. The Investigator
6. The Loyalist
7. The Enthusiast
8. The Challenger
9. The Peacemaker

Which are you? >>

People of a particular type have several characteristics in common, but they can be quite different nevertheless.

>>

WINGS

Usually one has characteristics of one of the types that lie adjacent to one's own that are more prominent. This is called the wing. So someone who is a type 5, might have a 4 wing or a 6 wing. This may be abbreviated to "5w4" and "5w6". If one doesn't have a dominant wing, it is said that the wings are balanced

Type 1

Perfectionists, responsible, fixated on improvement

Ones are essentially looking to make things better, as they think nothing is ever quite good enough. This makes them perfectionists who want to reform and improve, who desire to make order out of the omnipresent chaos.

Type 2

Helpers who need to be needed.

Twos essentially feel that they are worthy insofar as they are helpful to others. Love is their highest ideal. Selflessness is their duty.

Giving to others is their reason for being.

Involved, socially aware, usually extroverted, Twos are the type of people who remember everyone's birthday and who go the extra mile to help out a co-worker, spouse or friend in need.

Type 3

Focused on the presentation of success, to attain validation.

Threes need to be validated in order to feel worthy; they pursue success and want to be admired. They are frequently hard working, competetive and are highly focused in the pursuit of their goals, whether their goal is to be the most successful salesman in the company or the "sexiest" woman in their social circle.

Type 4

Identity seekers, who feel unique and different.

Fours build their identities around their perception of themselves as being somehow different or unique; they are thus self-consciously individualistic. They tend to see their difference from others as being both a gift and a curse - a gift, because it sets them apart from those they perceive as being somehow "common," and a curse, as it so often seems to separate them from the simpler forms of happiness that others so readily seem to enjoy.

Type 5

Thinkers who tend to withdraw and observe.

Fives essentially fear that they don't have enough inner strength to face life, so they tend to withdraw, to retreat into the safety and security of the mind where they can mentally prepare for their emergence into the world. Fives feel comfortable and at home in the realm of thought. They are generally intelligent, well read and thoughtful and they frequently become experts in the areas that capture their interest.

Type 6

Conflicted between trust and distrust.

Sixes essentially feel insecure, as though there is nothing quite steady enough to hold onto. At the core of the type Six personality is a kind of fear or anxiety. Sixes don't trust easily; they are often ambivalent about others, until the person has absolutely proven herself, at which point they are likely to respond with steadfast loyalty.

Type 7

Pleasure seekers and planners, in search of distraction.

Sevens are essentially concerned that their lives be an exciting adventure. They are future oriented, restless people who are generally convinced that something better is just around the corner. They are quick thinkers who have a great deal of energy and who make lots of plans. They tend to be extroverted, multi-talented, creative and open minded.

Type 8

Taking charge, because they don't want to be controlled.

Eights are essentially unwilling to be controlled, either by others or by their circumstances; they fully intend to be masters of their fate. Eights are strong willed, decisive, practical, tough minded and energetic.

They also tend to be domineering; their unwillingness to be controlled by others frequently manifests in the need to control others instead.

Type 9

Keeping peace and harmony.

Nines essentially feel a need for peace and harmony. They tend to avoid conflict at all costs, whether it be internal or interpersonal. As the potential for conflict in life is virtually ubiquitous, the Nine's desire to avoid it generally results in some degree of withdrawal from life, and many Nines are, in fact, introverted. Other Nines lead more active, social lives, but nevertheless remain to some to degree "checked out," or not fully involved, as if to insulate themselves from threats to their peace of mind.

Now that you have learned the Enneagram types.

Let us introduce you to your customized prayer journal >>

In the journaling pages we have pulled a verse and study questions for you to meditate on each morning. Each verse has been curated to envoke and stir reflection to your specific Ennaegram type.

Read and Respond on the lines,
Enjoy the Journey >>

Philippians 4:13

I can do all things through him who strengthens me.

Him > Me.

12-1-20

Jesus, thank you for calling me to reflect on your word! For really working in and through me to surrender for you to make good on your promise to make me new not by my effort but by yours! Jesus it is not by my strength but by yours! And in yours I CAN DO all things for your strength never fails! Jesus help me to live a joyful and dependant life in you! Please Holy Spirit give me grace to ask Stop and ask Why MORE! To be intentional about coming to you every moment of every day and bringing my full self to you! Align my heart with the truth of the Gospel! Open my heart and remove the armor that I do not want to hinder my precious time w/ you! Jesus crucify my flesh that I do not run to fleshy things for comfort but to you! I love you and trust you Jesus! Tn Jesus name I pray, Amen!

Isaiah 41:10

Fear not, for I am with you; be not dismayed, for I am your God; I will strengthen you, I will help you, I will uphold you with my righteous right hand.

12-2-20

Jesus, I feel like a bundle of nerves at times. Thank you that this is where you lead me today! Thank you Father that You strengthen me, You help me, You uphold me with Your righteous right hand. Jesus please align my heart with this truth, Your truth by Your spirit! Jesus I love you & worship you! This evening has been some weird and wild emotions! Please guide my heart & know I can trust my heart in Your, I need Your Holy Spirit to guide, lead and make me into the image of Jesus and what a hard but glorious process Jesus I am striving for my best creation unlike everyone! Please look down over me and use me that others will be changed through this tool that points them closer to You, I love you & trust You! & will abide in Your Spirit! In Jesus name I pray, Amen

Deuteronomy 31:6

Be strong and courageous. Do not fear or be in dread of them, for it is the Lord your God who goes with you. He will not leave you or forsake you.

12-31-20

Jesus thank you for the reassurance and promise of Your faithfulness! Thank You that I can trust you Lord! There are things I do fear, help me to rely on You more fully! Speak to and through me! Use me as a vessel to declare Your promises all the more! I wish I was more brave, and that I was strong and courageous! Help me to remember how Spirit I am only able to be those things in You! It is You who are those things. It is not and will never be me on my own! Jesus, please teach me and help me learn all I need to and can to help others along their hard journey. You! Teach me! Grow me! Use me! I fear failing at this... what if I am not strong enough? You are my strength and I will be strong and courageous! I love you and trust You! I will abide in You Jesus!
In Jesus name I pray, Amen

Isaiah 40:31

But they who wait for the Lord shall renew their strength; they shall mount up with wings like eagles; they shall run and not be weary; they shall walk and not faint.

12-4-20

Jesus thank you for this promise! Lord its hard to wait sometimes! But how wonderful and beautiful to do so! Jesus help me to know how to wait for you. Renew my strength, mount up with wings like eagles, help me run and not be weary, to walk and not faint! I need you Jesus! I need your love and your strength. I so desire to meet my future wife! Please bring us together! I miss this woman I haven't even met! I trust you and I love you! Let your will be done! Jesus carry me through the emergency certification! Teach me help me remember all I need to help others see themselves with astounding clarity to be free from self condemnation, fear and shame. And to accept your love, forgiveness and worth for I have done nothing before. I do love and trust you Jesus, I will abide in you Jesus. In Jesus name I pray, Amen!

1 Corinthians 10:13

No temptation has overtaken you that is not common to man. God is faithful, & He will not let you be tempted beyond your ability, but with the temptation he will also provide the way of escape, that you may be able to endure it.

12-5-20

Jesus, thank you for this promise, that your word stands true, forever!!! Father show me how you provide a way out that I may be able to endure the temptations in my life! I know I will stand for your will and ever able to make me stand! It's not based on what I do but on you have done and one day Jesus I am ready to meet my future bride! Open the doors to her, bring us together I want to meet her and spend time with her and get to know her. Jesus please help me, teach me your love and help me love others better! Guide me as I preach the evangium, help me make an impact in the lives of students! Use me! help me point to the Gospel and help others see the truth of your word! Open my heart. I love you, Jesus Lord Jesus I will await you. In Jesus name I pray, Amen!

Exodus 15:2

The Lord is my strength and my song, and he has become my salvation; this is my God, and I will praise him, my father's God, and I will exalt him.

12/6/20

Jesus! You alone are worthy of honor and glory and praise. I love you! Teach me, show me, guide me, lead me. You are my salvation, my life, my song! I praise you, for I am fearfully and wonderfully made. Jesus! Move my life forward according to your will! My heart despairs apart from you! But I am yours! You have declared you will never leave me or forsake me! I believe you, Lord! Jesus help me learn and grow as I learn about being an evergreen Christ. Train me to speak life into the lives of others by speaking the truth of the gospel and use this tool to guide them! Jesus! Please bring my future bride! Grow us closer together! Bless our meeting and our friendship! Please Jesus help us find one another! In Jesus name I pray! I love you and trust you Jesus! Shine Lord redeem me Jesus! Amen.

Ephesians 6:10

Finally, be strong in the Lord and in the strength of his might.

12-7-20

Abide, that is always what it points back to. Right to You! Jesus help me to abide in Your strength, Your wisdom, Your joy, Your will, Your love, Your life, Your peace! I can't have these things apart from You but only with You. Jesus please guide me, train me, lead me! Help me to help others today, you know their needs and fears. To assume their hearts as you do. Help me give away this tool a gift. And help me to start a business and do this thing right! Help me to have the time and resources to meet with people. Jesus I also ask that in Your strength please bring my future bride! Like Elisabeth pray and look and prepare me! Please bring her to me! Bless our meeting, our friendship and pursuit! You got her! I love knowing/trusting You Jesus! Help me to be near You Jesus! In Jesus name I pray. Amen!

Deuteronomy 20:4

For the Lord your God is he who goes with you to fight for you against your enemies, to give you the victory.

12-8-20

Thank you Jesus, victor over death and sin, Death where is your sting? For the Lord my God has come to fight for me and with me! Pt 3 You O Lord my God! Pt is You my King, Lord of my heart, to you I surrender my whole being, You go before me! You make me rise like on the wings of eagles, You make me run and not grow weary or faint! Jesus, guide me as I learn the enneagram content, make me wiser for this business to help people and churches grow and unite in your love! Jesus please bring my sister to bride and partner! Help us work together with you! Bless our meeting and grow center for you and teach us that I love you and serve Jesus! I will abide in you God! In Jesus name I pray, Amen!

2 Corinthians 12:9-10

But he said to me, "My grace is sufficient for you, for my power is made perfect in weakness." Therefore I will boast all the more gladly of my weaknesses, so that the power of Christ may rest upon me. For the sake of Christ, then, I am content with weaknesses, insults, hardships, persecutions, and calamities. For when I am weak, then I am strong.

12-9-20

Holy Spirit thank you for showing me true meaning of this passage that Weakness made to ~~you~~ in my weakness, You Lord God show up in your strength! Jesus I need you, I am frail and unable. Without you my situation at heart is unable but with you God all things are possible! Jesus I want to do and write ~~~~ a podcast! I want to coach people! I want to meet with chicks and companies! Where do I start? Where do you want ~~me~~ me to start? Guide me Lord, Show me your love, your life and presence in this! Please guide me Jesus! Bring me ~~cues~~ and use me to bring others to you to experience transformation with you! Please allow me to see it! Jesus! Please bless and bring my future husband! Bless our meeting and be glorified! I love you and trust you Jesus! I will abide in you Jesus! In Jesus name I pray, Amen!

Joshua 1:9

Have I not commanded you? Be strong & courageous. Do not be frightened, and do not be dismayed, for the Lord your God is with you wherever you go.!!!

12·10·20

Jesus! Mighty God, Prince of Peace, everlasting Savior! I can walk with my head held high for You are with me! You have called me to be strong and courageous. Your grace is sufficient for me! When I am weak Yahweh is strong! Jesus please push through every barrier in my life and my heart! Open every door! Make new neural pathways in my mind! Transform me in the image of your Son Father! Holy Spirit help me remember what I have learned and bring it to mind! Help me continue to learn and grow into my coach! Give me wisdom! Jesus as you transform me, please bless and bring my future bride! Bless our needs and bring us together! Not to carry for our good but for the good of others and Your glory Father! Bless my training and make me an advocate for my clients. Bring my clients and help me to point them to You! I love You and trust You Jesus! I will abide in You as You abide in me Jesus! In Jesus name I pray, Amen.

2 Timothy 1:7

For God gave us a spirit not of fear but of power and love and self-control.

12-11-20

Jesus, Thank you, Thank you, Thank you, for my day! Even though in the midst of chaos I thought it was hopeless... You came and not only kept my feet from stumbling but blessed me with Your favor, love and presence! Thank you Holy Spirit for hearing my prayer and aligning my heart not by my power but Yours! Please continue to align me. I know I may stray everyday but every day You will come through for me, I surrender all to You Jesus! Thank you Jesus that I passed the enneagram assessment! I am a certified enneagram coach! Thank You for how bright & strong that I read to be my day! Jesus please help me to use this tool to help others awaken to your love, truth and freedom that's only found in you! Jesus, Please bless, protect and bring my future bride! Bless our meeting and grow our friendship and love for one another! Align our hearts both yours and their behavior! I love you and trust you Jesus! I will abide in you as you abide in me Jesus! In Jesus name I pray Amen

Isaiah 12:2

Behold, God is my salvation; I will trust, and will not be afraid; for the Lord God is my strength and my song, and he has become my salvation.

12-13-20

Jesus my King! You are my salvation! You are my strength and my song! When I am weak, then I AM (Christ)/YAHWEH is strong! I praise you O'God! Father humble you for sending Jesus, and sealing my life with your Holy Spirit! I love you. I trust you! I praise you! Jesus I need your help, I don't have the strength for tomorrow. Please lead and guide me! I need you. Focus my heart, Holy Spirit al"ign my heart in/to the truth of the Gospel! Help me point others to you tomorrow! Please point both Thea and James to Yourself! Your love and Your heart, plans and purpose for them! Help me remember all you desire me to, all I need to. Jesus I ask for blessings over my future bride! Bless our meeting! Bring us together! Unite us with You. I love and trust you Jesus! I will abide in You as You abide in me Jesus! In Jesus name I pray, Amen

Matthew 11:28

Come to me, all who labor and are heavy laden, and I will give you rest.

12·13·20

Jesus! I am weary from my beloved heavy laden! I come to you because apart from you I can do NO good thing! And yet I find my heart wandering away! I come to you for rest Jesus! Jesus I have not remembered to abide in you! Please forgive me! I will abide in you Jesus as you abide in me and hold me and you will never let me go! Create new neural pathways in my mind! Holy Spirit, make my like Jesus! Be pure Lord, for I cannot do it alone! Jesus thank you for helping me learn all I have so far! Teach me to help others by leading them to you! Thank you for such a good session with Tom and please bless my session with James! Bring him and help him commit! Guide us through it! Jesus bless my future bride and bring us together, not because I'm good enough but because you are a good Father! I love you and trust you Jesus! I will abide in you as you abide in me, Jesus. In Jesus' name I pray, Amen

Isaiah 40:29

He gives power to the faint, and to him who has no might he increases strength.

12-15-20

Jesus I forgot to write last night I been busy & forgot to spend this time with you. Please forgive me Lord! I love this time, thank you I even came before you and be here with you! I needed this today! I'm having up to my fear of failure and steady out our starting this business! Father you hold all things together and there is no need to fear. You got this Jesus! Thank you for helping me keep as much as I have! Lead me Jesus! Knowing my heart for myself! Please let what I give be wise needing my paycheck! I am worried about that! Please help me to trust you more with this and not get too worked up! Jesus bless my church and bring new people! Help me to be able to make money from this! Help me to be able to really start this business Lord Jesus! Please bless my future fiance Bryn as together! Bless our meeting! I look forward to his blessing family yet! I love you and I trust you Jesus, I will abide in you as you abide in me. Jesus in Jesus name I pray, Amen!

Psalm 27:1

Of David. The Lord is my light and my salvation; whom shall I fear? The Lord is the stronghold of my life; of whom shall I be afraid?

12-16-20

Jesus, thank you for Pouring over me! I praise you O'Lord for I am fearfully and wonderfully made! Lord Jesus you redeem all things, redeem my heart O'God! Change my life, I surrender it to you! Jesus help me please renew and transform my, why?! Why I am I spending? Why am I doing? Why am I saying? Why am I thinking? Holy Spirit create new neural pathways in my mind! Lead me Jesus! Holy Spirit Please mold me into the likeness of Jesus! Help me coach people help me give it away and help me meet those who will pay for my services. Jesus use this tool to transform lives and bring glory to the Father! Help me start a business! Bless my federal tax ide! Bring for lead people please who is in need! I love you and I trust you Jesus! I will walk on in Jesus as You've made done! In Jesus name I pray, Amen!

Psalm 31:24

Be strong, and let your heart take courage, all you who wait for the Lord!

12·17·20

Jesus! I don't feel strong, yet you declare me to be! I am not who I want to be! I look and gaze at what I don't want to. I allow my heart to misalign with your truth! Holy Spirit please shift my heart back onto alignment. Please open new neural (pathways?) I don't want to be the same! I want to be the man you've called me to be! Jesus forgive my broken thoughts and my heart wanting to be seen/my own laziness/run others way instead of you! Please guide my heart! Jesus guide me into the right business! Open my heart to your will and guide me!
Bless my future bride, bring us together! I want to pursue her, & pursue her. I want to love her and have sex with her! I want to experience intimacy both her & yours with her. Please Jesus! Bless my ministry, ...

Psalm 73:26

My flesh and my heart may fail, but God is the strength of my heart and my portion forever.

12/18/80

Jesus this world has and does fail me. My flesh and my will has and does fail me. But you Lord Jesus! And of my heart NEVER DO! Praise you Jesus! Jesus on my mind right now is/today this business, and debt and failure or at least the fear of it! Jesus & buy each one of these things at your feet! You who came as a human to save me. Who is victor over our life and death! & lay them at your feet! Jesus & put my heart in your hands. Please Father if it is your will please help me get the domain of cbride gospel enmeagram curchcom! This means so much to me! Please Jesus, please open this door! O Lord open this door! Make a way! Please help me to get a bgo made for cheap too! But a good quality! Jesus bless my future bride! Bring her, bless our meetings! I love you and & thank you Jesus! & I love to serve you as I've abided in you Jesus! In Jesus name & power, Amen!

2 Corinthians 12:9

But he said to me, "My grace is sufficient for you, for my power is made perfect in weakness." Therefore I will boast all the more gladly of my weaknesses, so that the power of Christ may rest upon me.

12/14/20

Jesus! You are so loving! I have always looked at this verse as a "NO" but it is actually a "YES" just not in the way I expected! For your grace is sufficient for all my needs. With your grace you give the gospel to me. By your grace, you woke me up, you adopted me and you transform me! Given the lies I've been told of thoughts, lose their power over me when you throw your grace over me & power over me when I lead. Jesus! I love you! Please continue to do wonders for this coming business. I love you, I praise you! Thank you for the domain generally both the logo and the art/brand LLC. Give it to whoever needs to grow it. According to your will given it! Jesus please bless my future bride! Bring her and bring us together! Take away Jesus! Bring us unity! Jesus I am and I trust you! I will trade up you Jesus as you didn't with me I ...

Mark 12:30

And you shall love the Lord your God with all your heart and with all your soul and with all your mind and with all your strength.

12·20·10

What an honor O'Lord to have You with ALL OF ME! Jesus thank you for connecting me to yourself! I need you Jesus, please grow me, mature me! Holy Spirit align my heart with the truth of the Gospel! Create new neural pathways in my mind! Get me out of my old way of thinking! Save me! Jesus please help me start this business! Not only start it but to see peoples lives changed by seeing themselves clearly and surrendering to your truth and the Gospel! Help me connect this week with others. Rachel and Emily and help me to ~~start~~ connect with them and start having ~~sessions~~ with them Lord! Trust turn them! Jesus I ~~do want to start~~ being able to make payments as well! Help me make money Lord Jesus! Bring to be my future bride! Bring us together! Bless our meeting! I love you so much Lord Jesus! Truth to be with you Jesus just now let's do it me! Encouragement & joy, Amen

Nehemiah 8:10

Then he said to them, "Go your way. Eat the fat and drink sweet wine, and send portions to anyone who has nothing ready, for this day is holy to our Lord. And do not be grieved, for the joy of the Lord is your strength."

Dec 21, 20

Jesus! Thank you for letting me be apart of Life Change! Growing my heart and desire to see peoples lives blessed and enriched by your trust in my love! Jesus I have spent alot of money! Please help me to be able to pay off this card and credit totally in less than a year! Help me to get out of debt and help others connect more deeply. Help me to change lives with you and not only preach even but to be a profit! Please bring paying clients that I can coach! Jesus make money! make money where there is no way! Please help me coach others according to your will! Please be you in coach Gigi! I love you and I praise you! I ask all this not in my will but in your will Father! Bless my future bride! Bring us together and bless our meeting! you are everything to me as are I love you and I trust you Jesus! I will make sure Jesus as I hold to your's
in Jesus name I pray, Amen!

Psalm 46:1

To the choirmaster. Of the Sons of Korah. According to Alamoth. A Song. God is our refuge and strength, a very present help in trouble.

12-22-20

Jesus! I got so upset at Theo's comment. How could anyone think science doubt/negate prove your existence? You are God! All things point to you, my very existence cries out that you are God! Open my heart not to be so hard on or opposed to my brother. What righteous fury I feel. Please forgive me lord! Help me to speak rightly. Jesus I started the website today! It looks pretty good overall but still needs work. Please guide me with. Help me to write more on the beliefs and on setup the small things like scheduling. Jesus! Guide me because I don't know what I'm doing. Help me to get some focus on what you bring to my heart. Please bring me clients who you need me/want to contact them with love. Help me to have an open heart. Jesus we pray to bring you my best everyday. Please bring my future bride, bless our purity. Onwards together I commend/commit/trust you Jesus. In Jesus' name we pray. Amen

Habakkuk 3:19

God, the Lord, is my strength; he makes my feet like the deer's; he makes me tread on my high places. To the choirmaster: with stringed instruments.

12.23.20

O' Jesus! How I praise your name! Keep my eyes open every day King! I love you! Father thank you for your love and desire to be with me! To know me and that I know you! Holy Spirit make me like Jesus! Bring me more in the image of my Lord and King Jesus! I will make room for you to do whatever you want to! I lay it all down before you, I give you my best and ask that you use me! For the work I do is done by the enablement of your Holy Spirit! Please help me want anything I should have ready! Jesus please guide the building of this business and use it to glorify Jesus and yourself Father! Please Father bring me clients and use me to point them to you! Jesus please bless my future bride! Bless our meeting, bringing us together and grow us together! I love you and I trust you Jesus! I will look unto you Jesus as you alone are all I need & desire now & forever, Amen!

Psalm 29:11

May the Lord give strength to his people! May the Lord bless his people with peace!

12.24.30

Thank you Lord Jesus for such a Sunday! Thank you for filling me with Your Spirit! Your love, hope, joy, peace and strength! Strengthen my resolve! Use me O Lord, guide me, lead me! I lay myself, this business, this ministry all at Your feet! Use and grow it all as you see fit! Take all of me Lord and use me as a vessel to build Your Kingdom! Use my testimony and my message, talents, gifts and all to reach people with You! Jesus bring people to me to coach, use me as a compass to point to You! Jesus please bring income in, please pay this credit card down with me! Take all of my resources and use them as you see fit! Lead me Holy Spirit and glorify the Father and Jesus name! Please bless my future bride, bring us closer as together! Bless our needs and grow us together! I love you and trust you Jesus! Such a lovely day Jesus as You would have! Encouragement spirit, Amen

John 16:33

I have said these things to you, that in me you may have peace. In the world you will have tribulation. But take heart, I have overcome the world.

12-25-20

Jesus, Merry Christmas! Thank you for such a wonderful Christmas day with you! Hiking and spending time in prayer and solitude was the best Christmas morning! And playing with the kids was fun! I love you Lord! Thank you for rest, for solitude and for fun times with others! Jesus as I go to bed & rest for good rest. Prepare my heart for my session with Yolanda tomorrow at 10am and my consultation with Saul tomorrow! Please guide me in starting this business, bring clients to me, paying clients. Help me start off right. Help me do it well! Jesus I need you, your help and direction. Lord help me write a mission statement, use me, lead me, grow me, send me! Help me start content for presentations and Facebook! Jesus please bless my future brides, bring her Lord. Bless our meeting, growing together! Jesus I love you and trust you! Jesus & I will do and be Jesus' hands & feet & Jesus name & pray, Amen

1 Peter 4:11

Whoever speaks, as one who speaks oracles of God; whoever serves, as one who serves by the strength that God supplies—in order that in everything God may be glorified through Jesus Christ. To him belong glory & dominion forever and ever. Amen.

12-26-20

Jesus you are the supplier of all my needs and desires! O how I praise you O'God! Thank you for not only meeting all my needs but supplying all of my needs as well! God create new neural pathways in my mind! Guide me, lead me, send me, use me! Renew my mind and transform for your purpose and your plans! Holy Spirit make me like Jesus! Bless the coaching & gift todo! Please guide me! Bring me clients and bring together all that I need! Help me Prepare the discovery/survey/design presentation and work through! Jesus please bring these things together in me! Gui da dhy heart! Please work out that & may present to Rev and other Churches/organizations. Please Jesus bless my future bride! Bring us together! Bless our meeting and grow us together! Slave I want & trust you Jesus! I will labor de in you as you abide in me Jesus. In Jesus name I pray, Amen!

Matthew 6:33

But seek first the kingdom of God and his righteousness, and all these things will be added to you.

12-27-20

Jesus! I see your love and your heart for me and others! I want everyone to experience freedom in you! I love you and I praise you! Holy Spirit please help me to seek first the kingdom of God and His righteousness! Help me to align my heart to yours, Holy Spirit align my heart with the truth of the Gospel! I want everyone to feel freedom in you Jesus. What would you have me do? Love my people. I will Lord! Jesus please bless my meeting with Jimmy tomorrow and my session with Aaron and Hannah on Tuesday! Please help me to serve those I coach to prosper and give my best! Help me restore faith in the with you, others and myself! Help me build this business! Help me prepare a presentation! Help me to file for my LLC. and help me to prepare for your work in this thing! Please bless my future brother Jesus! Bring us together! Bless my meeting tomorrow to

Psalm 23:4

Even though I walk through the valley of the shadow of death, I will fear no evil, for you are with me; your rod and your staff, they comfort me.

12/28/20

Jesus my good shepherd! My comforter! Please forgive me for what you are doing! Open my heart and align my heart with the truth of the Gospel. Lord this is not something I can do on my own, I need you to do it in me! Thank you for using me. Thank you for allowing me to witness the changes in Tim, James, Yolanda, Leslie, Amy's & will see in Sarah and Aaron and Hannah! Seeing and being a part of what you are doing is healing! Jesus please make a way! Jesus guide me, lead me, use me, send me! Make me new! Jesus, Father, Holy Spirit, O God, my God! Please bless the business! Please guide and bless me as I navigate it! Lord please bring paying clients. Please guide me through it all. Please help me get good reviews and most of all please bless and give blessings to those I counsel. Jesus please bless my future wife, marriage & together! Bless our meeting and courtship by faith!! I love you and trust you Jesus! I will obey! Amen! Jesus as I praise you, I will praise your name Spirit, Sweet

2 Timothy 4:17

But the Lord stood by me and strengthened me, so that through me the message might be fully proclaimed and all the Gentiles might hear it. So I was rescued from the lion's mouth.

12.29.20

Praise Your name o'Lord! You are not just faithful to me but everyone! You desire all to be saved and brought to You! Thank You Father! Guide me, lead me, use me, sustain! Please Jesus help me reach people for Your Kingdom! Help me to help others see themselves in order to more deeply align their hearts with You! Holy Spirit guide our hearts more deeply! I love You Lord! I want others to experience true freedom in You like You gave me! Thank You for a few days rest from coaching! Please help me to get everyone settled in this process You have given us! Please help Rachel surrender and feel real change by surrendering to You in Jesus' name every day! Please grow this business! Please help me pay off this credit card! Provide the money Lord please! Open every door! Help me! Buy paying clients! Jesus please bless my future bride, how we're together! Bless us really growing together! I love You and trust You Jesus! I will also remember Jesus as God God has done! In Jesus name I pray, Amen

Psalm 118:14

The Lord is my strength and my song; he has become my salvation.

12-30-20

Praise to you O'Lord my God! You are my salvation, I could never do it on my own! I had try to even when I'm not trying. Jesus please forgive my wandering eyes and heart! Holy Spirit please realign my heart with the truth of the Gospel! Jesus please guide me, lead me, change me where, send me! Holy Spirit make me into the image of Jesus! Grow my heart and set my feet on the path! Thank you for providing space to put together the presentation. Please help me to put together a custom one! Jesus please help me us & our starting this business, there is still some to do! Please help me to know what to do! Where to go or where to list online! Jesus open the door! Thank you for the stumbles even! Even being able to post little reminders on the CC was great! Help me use the planner and help me to be more intentional with it! Jesus please bless my future today, bring her to you! Bless everyone I care to help! Jesus & bring peace & the truth! Jesus will continue in a reasonable manner! In Jesus name I pray, Amen

2 Thessalonians 3:3

But the Lord is faithful. He will establish you and guard you against the evil one.

12-3-20

Jesus thank you for this promise and reminder! You not only establish me but guard me from the evil one! Because You are faithful! Lord Jesus please guard my heart and transform me into Your likeness! Holy Spirit create new neural pathways in my mind! Change me, guide me, lead me, use me, send me! Jesus please bless my consultation with Rachel tomorrow! Please let her be my first paid client, but Father not my will but Yours be done! Thank you for leading me to complete the presentation and just creating social media content! Thank You for 2020! So much has happened and truly You know and one day I will know they! & Praise Your name O Lord! Guide me into what You have next! Help me fully establish this business, as social media presence and after cost! Please help me to do SEOs and more and change my life! Must Bless my future wife my Lord! Please bring her in 2021, long suffering, blessed, reading and growing! I love You and trust You Jesus! I will be thankful as I obedience Jesus! In Jesus name I pray, Amen.

PRAYERS ANSWERED

CONGRATULATIONS YOU MADE IT THROUGH THE 30 DAYS.

PLEASE SHARE YOUR JOURNEY WITH US.

enneagramjournal.co

Made in the USA
Coppell, TX
29 November 2020

42440813R00056